The Great Game

How lessons from the great game of golf can help you win the, equally great, game of business

Kevin Stansfield

Cover image by: 418 Limited
Book design by: SWATT Books Ltd

Printed in the United Kingdom

ISBN 978-1-7398481-0-1 (Paperback)

Kinetics Publishing
East Wellow
SO51 6AZ

www.kinetics-uk.com

*For all the slicers, hookers, chokers &
yippers in golf, business and life.*

"Golf is not a game of perfect."
Dr Bob Rotella

"Golf, business and life are not games of perfect"
Kevin Stansfield

Praise for *The Great Game*

The Great Game is a brilliant approach to business and a real easy way to digest some key business lessons. It might even improve my golf!

– Tyler Everitt, Kingfisher Plc

I really enjoyed reading your book which highlighted some excellent comparisons between golf and business. I particularly liked the chapter on the four types of players and having fun learning to become better versions of ourselves. There are certainly lots of golden nuggets to help me with my golf and my business in the future. A great read.

– Carolyn Williams, Nutmeg Property Sourcing Ltd

Kevin has done a brilliant job of taking the game of golf, the training and the outcomes and showing how we can use these approaches to improve our business performance. He shows with just some simple changes to our business strategy, in the same way that one would do to improve the game of golf, we can shift the focus and perform better. Every aspect of the game is linked to the world of business and certainly I took away some great ideas and ways to approach business processes and success.

— Steve Woods, The Golf Performance Hypnotist

I found this book very interesting and a very different approach of marrying golf with business. As a self-employed business owner of 11 years and a keen golfer, it is the best of both Worlds and I picked up many tips. A very good read.

— David Hatmil, Tender Assist Limited

It's amazing how incredibly linked business and golf is . A great read for golfers and business people alike!!

— Bob Grace, WPA Healthcare Practice PLC

As an avid frustrated but addicted golfer the alignment to business is cruelly uncanny. This book is an enthralling read with a blend of so many relevant observations and fresh learnings. Read the section on courses and I defy you to not identify with the journey. This book will endure and find a place in the boardrooms and classrooms of the future, in equal measure!

— James Filmer, Tier One Worldwide

I have read the Great Game with interest as I am a keen golfer and have had some interesting business experiences in my life. I wish I had read it when I was just starting out in business and in golf. There is no doubt that learning to do things the right way before you start is better than trial and error. Setting goals and measuring against them is essential for improvement but you have to want to improve in the first place. This book is definitely worth a read for anyone in business who wishes to do better.

— Thomas Olesen, My Local

Loved the book and in many parts could have been writing about me. Would have been great to have this available a few years back, but never too old to step back and take a fresh look at yourself and your business.

– David Marshall, My Brand Group Limited

Great book showing how golf and business are aligned in so many ways. Chapter 10 is one of my favourites, 'The Mind', which gives a very clear understanding and interesting insight into the mindset for golf and business. An excellent read.

– Mark Amey, Golf Professional

The Great Game Book is a fantastic book. I am from a family of golfers. My mother and father met at a golf club. My brother became a scratch player, golfing around the world and a member of the Royal and Ancient.
So, this book really resonated with me. My father always thought that business and golf were games that worked so well together, and this book is inspired in its analogies between the two.
A great read, and everything covered, including the essential 19th hole. A must read for anyone chasing business and balls around the golf course.

– Robert Duncan, Cartoonist

The Great Game draws on the similarities, in such an insightful way, between running a business and playing the game of golf. As a businessman and club golfer I can vouch that anyone like me will benefit from the teachings of this very interesting and thoroughly enjoyable book. Furthermore, any non-golfing business owner who reads this book will quite possibly feel the desire to start playing the great game of golf.

– Gordon E. Starkey,
Global Brand Ambassador for regia-timepieces.com

This book contains powerful metaphors and links between golf and business that we can all understand and build from. Having worked for over 25 years from the other direction training golfers to help others play better golf I have borrowed much of that from the business world. Reading this book will bring clarity to both games, in a very enjoyable fashion.

– Peter Hudson, World Golf Teachers Federation

Contents

Foreword

In my many years of coaching people, both in a business and sporting world, I have heard so many times people refer to themselves or others as "having potential", that it has virtually lost its meaning. Does having potential motivate you, does it make you get up and do things that no other person would do?

I have therefore, come to the conclusion that it is not potential that we have, but a hidden genius that is waiting to be unlocked. Genius refers to the innate abilities of each and every individual – it means that we all have the resources, skills and abilities to achieve in something, we just have to discover what that something could be.

There are many arenas in which people strive to fulfil their genius, and sport is one that we can all relate to. All sports are relatively simple. You know what it takes to win before you start playing the game. You know who the opposition are, the rules are written down and are fair to all who play and there are always people who have played the game before willing to show you how to play it to the best of your ability and bring out your hidden genius.

Business on the other hand is an arena in which achieving your genius is not as simple to see or do. People come into business for many reasons, and many get lost along the way. They become too busy dealing with the everyday, caught up in the vital maintenance of the business, and fail to unlock their true genius or to see that there's another way to play the game. One that is more effective, more productive, more fulfilling, and much more likely to deliver the spoils of victory, much more quickly.

Kevin's choice of golf to compare with business is inspired, as it is one of the sports that is played as much in the mind as it is on the course. By drawing clear parallels between golf and business, Kevin brilliantly demystifies and simplifies what it takes to unlock your true genius and use it to be successful in these two "Great Games".

Myles Downey
Author & Coach

Introduction

My experience of golf and business started at about the same time. When I was 12, my father gave up his job as a financial controller for the Dover Harbour Board, and bought a sign company from a man in a pub. After a year or so, he decided to join the local golf and country club. Neither of us had played golf before, but I suppose he felt that it was what business people do.

We had a great couple of years there - we had some lessons, bought some clubs and I think played together for about 12 months until he hurt his back, and could no longer play.

He kept the membership for another year, but then the business hit a bad patch and he stopped, and so did my golf.

After that, I played once or twice a year when I was invited to play with mates, but I never really got into the game until I was in my early 40s.

As for my career, I chose not to join my father in his business venture. Our relationship had deteriorated during my teenage years. He spent all his time working in the business, and now that his bad back prevented him from playing sport, we had even less in common. Therefore, the thought of working for him was never there.

I did however decide to follow his lead and trained to become a Chartered Accountant. Once qualified, I moved to Southampton in the mid 1990s and subsequently worked with the owners of hundreds of small and medium sized businesses. Following this, I became a freelance Finance Director, and helped the businesses I was working with grow from a few million in sales, to hundreds of millions.

After taking a year out to undertake a Master of Business Administration (MBA) in 2006, I joined ActionCOACH, the world's #1 business coaching organisation.

During the last 15 years, I have coached over 250 business owners to help them grow their business, make more money and have more time. This was the main reason I started to play golf again. Many of my clients and prospective clients played, or wanted more free time to play this great game.

I re-started golf like most adults, who start later in their life, thinking that I could just pick up a club, take a swing, hit the ball and enjoy the game. At the time, I was playing tennis at a reasonable level, and have always been able to adapt to racket sports quickly, so surely, golf would be no different. But it was, big time.

Yes, I could hit a ball, but where it ended up varied from shot to shot. I used to think that a good shot was a result of my skill, but now I look back and realise that it was more luck.

Being at the top of your game as a Business Coach means investing time and money in your own education and keeping an open mind on new ideas and concepts. You find the best bits and relate them simply and effectively to your clients' businesses. Luckily, I have always loved learning, although those last few years of studying for my accounting exams were rather painful.

I think it's my love of learning that has kept me in coaching for so long. I am always learning, and my clients are always growing, so the challenges are different and the skills I need to employ are changing all the time. I will never get bored of it, and therefore I will play the game for a long time.

I took the same approach to golf. I wanted to be better at playing the game, so I started learning how to do it. I read books, watched videos, had group and 1:1 coaching. There were so many aspects to learn and perfect that I became a bit addicted to it. I would watch a YouTube video, then go to the range to practice. However, there were so many ways to approach the game, and I had such a random way of learning, that I soon got myself in a right mess and started to go backwards.

At this point, I had managed to get to a 9 handicap, which had been my target when I started on 18. Having achieved this, I wanted to be better, but knew that the swing I had was never going to get me there. So I had to start again, and this time do it properly.

It was this decision that made me look at the similarities between golf and business. Many of the business owners I had worked with over the years had built good businesses doing it their way. They didn't take any lessons before they started, and relied on hard work and changing tactics when things did not work. But after many years, they got themselves to the point where they could just not break through and achieve the success they desired.

"What got them here would not get them there"

This was just like me with my golf game. The difference was, I knew I had to go and see a golf professional to help me change.

Most business owners have no idea that professional business coaches exist.

As a result of this revelation, I set up, with my golf coach, my own golf and business networking group.

I would talk about a business concept and he would relate this topic to golf. We had a great few years, teaching people to play the 'Game of Business' and golf better, and enjoy both games more. The problem was, I never seemed to find enough people who enjoyed learning as much as I did. Lots of excuses were given, with "not enough time" being the most common one, and this got me thinking. Why is it, when everybody knows that to get better at something you have to put in the effort to learn, do so few people actually do so?

Too many amateur golfers look at a professional golfer and say, "I wish I could play like that". But they are saying the wrong thing. What they should really be saying is:

"I wish I could dedicate my life to something that I believe in as much as they do."

The same is true for people in business. They look at successful businesspeople like Richard Branson, Alan Sugar and Bill Gates, and ignore the fact that these people have dedicated their lives to building businesses that are way beyond something that just pays them a wage.

So, what about businesspeople who play golf? Well, most are unlikely to earn their fortune becoming professional golfers. And if we're being honest, they don't really want to build multi-billion pound business empires. But they do have the ability and, I believe, the desire to be better at both golf and business.

It is for this reason that I decided to write this book. I wanted to show the similarities in playing the games of golf and business, and how these can be used to help the reader enjoy both a little more than they do now, or maybe ever have.

If you have been recommended or given this book, it is because the donor sees you as one of those people who like to learn and better yourself. If you enjoy the book, please pass it on to another player. If you do not, then do let me know as I am always keen for feedback to improve.

If you have bought this book then I am pleased I have found somebody who loves to learn and I hope I give you at least one great idea to improve your golf, business and life as a whole.

Chapter 1: The Game

The first similarity between golf and business can be traced back to their origins. The modern game of golf can be traced back to 15th century Scotland, and some historians believe the ancient origins date back to Roman times in the first century BC.

People started making a living from golf alone in the mid 1800s and it could be argued that Old Tom Morris was one of the first professional players, winning the first Open Championship in 1860. The body that represents all professional players, The Professional Golfers' Association (PGA), was set up some 56 years later, in 1916.

The 'Game of Business' has similar roots. While people have bartered for goods for thousands of years, the concept of a separate business that trades in its own right came about in the 15th/16th century. The word 'Company' originates from the Latin 'Companio' – one who eats bread with you. The word came into its current use in the 16th century, when it was taken to mean a business association.

The first publicly traded stock was The Dutch East India Company in 1602, with the London Stock Exchange being formed in 1698. The first limited liability company (Ltd), which gave the shareholders legal protection from creditors, was set up in 1855.

So you can see that both 'games' have not only been around for a very long time, but have grown and evolved side by side for most of their lives, and while on the surface the modern versions are very different to their historic origins, underneath the principles on which they were built are very much the same.

The game of golf is very simple. The aim is to get a little white ball from the start of each hole into a little cup at the end of the hole, marked by a flag, in as few strokes as possible.

If you are running a business, you may not think it is as simple as a game of golf, but I think it can be expressed just as simply:

"The Game of Business is to create value to its customers at a profit to the owners of the business."

Now I agree that it can be bigger than this – add in corporate social responsibility for a start – but just as with golf, the fundamentals of the game really are this simple. The challenge is that, as humans, we have a great ability to overcomplicate simple things, and it is therefore a coach's responsibility to make the complicated simple enough for their client to understand and make appropriate changes.

I have boiled business and golf down into 12 chapters, each one focusing on a different part of the game and showing the similarities between golf and business, and how the lessons in one can help in the other. Let me start by running through each of these so you can see how we can break down the 'Game of Business' and the game of golf and what stops us from mastering them both.

The first area where things go wrong is not being clear on what the goal is. Both golf and business can mean different things to different people and if you don't understand your goal, you will face problems before you start. For me, this is the most important factor in any game, and I focus on this area in **Chapter 2 – The Goal**.

The next issue is, why you are playing the game in the first place? What type of player are you? If you know this, then you will get so much more out of the game. I have identified 4 types of players, which I will share with you in **Chapter 3 – The Players**.

While my simple definitions above of both games are fundamentally true, every course we play and business we run is different. Even the weather from one day to another can make a big impact on the game. It is these challenges that make the game so enduring. If every golf hole were identical and every business the same, we would tire of them very quickly and go and do something more exciting. For this reason, I look at the **Course, Hazards & Conditions** in **Chapters 4 & 5**.

The next area that can help us or hinder us is the equipment at our disposal to play the game better. Sometimes I think that if there was only one club in golf and one way to make a profit in business, life would be so much easier, but we have so many tools at our disposal. How to master these tools is covered in **Chapter 6 – The Clubs**.

Because so many people play these two games and we all have an inbuilt desire to win, sometimes at any cost, both games have had to adopt rules. These are not only to stop cheats from winning, but also to clarify difficult decisions, and keep the game as fair as possible. This is where the 'Game of Business' and golf might seem the most different, but I will show you why this is perhaps not the case in **Chapter 7 - The Rules**.

You can play the game of golf and business without knowing all the rules, but you cannot play either game without knowing how it is scored. While the overall score, in terms of shots and profits, is the goal, if you want to play the game at a high level you must know there are far more scores to keep track of. I show you these in **Chapter 8 - The Scorecard**.

Who you play your games with can make a massive difference to your success and enjoyment of the game. Imagine playing golf with the most miserable golfer in the club, day in and day out. You would soon give up or change clubs. So why do so many business owners carry on playing with these people in their businesses? I look further into this in **Chapter 9 - The Team**.

Probably the biggest factor in both games is the difference between the external game, i.e. the actions we take, and the internal game, i.e. how we think. Our brains are immensely powerful, and while they help us learn and perform well, they can also trip us up and cause great frustration. I have dedicated **Chapter 10 - The Mind**, to this major topic.

Getting help in playing a sport better is always seen as a strength. No top golf professional would dream of playing the game without a coach or caddie. While not as common in business, at the top-level, CEOs are coming round to the idea that they similarly need expert help to achieve their goals. **Chapter 11 - The Caddie/Coach**, shows you why this help is needed, and what to expect when you take on a coach.

Finally, like all games, there must be a time when we stop playing, and can enjoy a beer and chat with friends on how well we played. But while this is simple in golf, it is far from it in business, so my final **Chapter 12 - The 19th Hole**, gives you some insights on how this can be achieved.

I hope you can now start to see that the simplicity of both games starts to get clouded by the way we approach playing them. My intention for this book is to help you understand more about the business game you are playing and give you some insights into what you need to focus on, in order to play it better. After all, when you have built a business that works without you, you will have more time to work on your golf.

But before we start looking at how we play the game, let's start by looking at why we are playing it in the first place …

Chapter 2: The Goal

As we saw in Chapter 1, the goal of golf is to go around a course of 9 or 18 holes in as few shots as possible. This is unambiguous, simple to understand and probably why so many people play and enjoy the game. You could teach this concept to a 1-year-old, and in fact, Tiger Woods started swinging a golf club when he was 6 months old.

Every course has a par score which players attempt to beat, and every player is given a handicap based on how well they are currently playing the game. This allows the player not only to assess how well they are playing the game, but it also evens up the game, so people at different levels can play against each other.

Goals in golf are normally broken down into short-terms ones and long-term ones. Short term, it is about the player beating par, plus their handicap on the day they are playing, while for the long term it is about lowering their handicap.

The 'Game of Business', however, is not so simple. While the definition in Chapter 1 identifies maximisation of profits and customer value as the goal, only you as the business owner get to quantify what level this should be. In effect, you as the business owner get to set what 'par' is for your business.

The game is also made harder by the fact that you are competing with and against others playing the game, but they have got their own rule book, and run to a different 'par.' In addition, unlike golf, there is no handicap system to even up the playing field.

So, where do you start, when setting your goals in business? I think you do exactly as you do in golf. You have short-term achievable goals, i.e. a target profit figure, the equivalent of beating par, and long-term aspirational goals of what you want your business to look like in the future, the equivalent of your handicap.

To me all short-term goals should be SMART: Specific, Measurable, Achievable, Realistic in a Timeframe. They certainly are these things in golf. For example:

> *"Today, I would like to go round in under 90 and beat my friends. I can measure my progress every hole, I have shot under 90 before, so this is achievable, it is realistic to finally win something as I have been playing well recently and we are going to do this in under 4 hours."*

When I finish my round, I will know instantly if I have been successful or not. While failure is always a possibility, rarely does it put us off setting the goal or playing the game. We just accept that it is part of the fun, and tomorrow will be another day, with the chance to try for the goal again.

When setting your short-term business goals, the first thing you must do is set the timeframe you will be playing your game over. The starting timeframe will be a year, as this fits with the timeframe for your annual accounts for tax and filing at Companies House. But, in my mind, this is too long a period in which to play the 'Game of Business'. Imagine playing golf for over a year and not knowing your score or if you had won anything until a year had passed.

The beauty of golf and all sports is that even if the overall game could be over a year (golf's Race to Dubai or Fed Ex Cup) there are sub games that can be played and won on a more regular basis.

My recommendation is that after setting the annual sales and profit goals, you then break them down into quarterly, monthly or even weekly targets. You could even go down as far as daily and hourly targets, but more on that in Chapter 8 - The Score Card. The timeframe you use should fit in with the type of business you are running. For fast-moving sales businesses, e.g. cafés, retail and casinos, it would be OK to set daily and weekly goals, but this would not work for slower, bigger ticket sales such as construction or estate agents, who would be better with monthly or quarterly targets.

Once you have set your timeframe you can then set your specific and measurable goals. Your starting place should always be a cash goal or a profit goal, which relates back to the overall goal for the year. Personally I prefer profit goals, as cash is more fluid, but that does not mean you should ignore it.

Unfortunately, many businesses focus first on the sales goals, and profit becomes an afterthought, but this would be the same as focusing in golf on your driving and not the overall score. Remember that the only purpose of selling something is to make a profit.

Once you know your profit goal, then you must break this down into sub goals around the areas that make this up. Just as a golfer will break their round into fairways hit, greens in regulation and putts made, in business this would be sales, cost of sales and overheads. But even these can be broken down and goals set in areas such as leads, conversion rates, average £ sale value. I will leave the explanation of these to Chapter 8 – the Score Card.

The final part of successful goal-setting is to ensure your goal is achievable and realistic in relation to your current level of skill, and the time you have available. There is no point in setting a low par or high profit goal when deep down you know you don't have the skill or time to achieve it and then being upset when you fall short. Likewise, don't set a high par or low profit goal, because, while you will certainly achieve it, you may find yourself disappointed and ultimately demotivated when you do.

The key is to stretch yourself 10-20% beyond where you think you can get to. If you know you can shoot 90, set the goal for 80, because you will be more likely to hit 82 than if you had set the goal at 85. Likewise, if your best month's profit was £50k, stretch it to £60-70k. Above all, be honest with yourself and share your goals with somebody you trust and will give you honest feedback. This is why having a coach is a must, but I will leave that for Chapter 11 – The Caddie/Coach.

Short-term goals are only part of the game you are playing. You also need longer-term, aspirational goals. These will be more inspirational and emotional – think of them like dreams. In golf, this could be getting to single figure or scratch handicap, or playing all the top courses in the world. These goals don't have to be SMART, and you are unlikely to know how you are going to get there, but as they are long-term, as long as you have time and you continue to work towards them with your short-term goals, there is always a chance you will achieve them.

In business, aspirational goals will centre around what type of business you want to build, what you want it to achieve for you, and where do you personally want to be in 5 – 10 years' time.

Bradley J Sugars, Founder of ActionCOACH, serial entrepreneur and rather wealthy individual, says the ultimate goal of any business owner is to…

*"build a commercial, profitable enterprise
that will work without you."*

The reason this makes sense is that if your business relies on you, it is never really complete. You are still "HAVING" to work, so you have only created yourself a "JOB".

Now, there are many people with jobs who are more than happy and have a great life. But if you own or run a business, then it must be able to survive when you have gone.

Think of Ford disappearing when Henry Ford died, Apple ceasing to be when Steve Jobs died, or even Virgin being no more when Sir Richard Branson leaves this world. If this were to happen, the world would lambast them for not building their businesses so that they could continue to earn profit and create more value to their customers, after the founders had left.

For this reason, when I am starting work with a client for the first time, I will get them to think about where they want to be in 5-10 years' time. I ask them what income levels they want personally, and when they would like to sell the business or have it work without them. From this, we can calculate the level of profit that would be needed to achieve that future vision.

For example, if in 10 years you want to have an income of £50,000 per year while not having to work (passive income), you will need £1m of assets to invest at 5% Return on Investment (ROI), in order to achieve this. (£1m x 5% = £50k).

To get the £1m from your business you will either need to make £100,000 per year surplus profit every year for 10 years, and invest that, or you will need to build the business so you can sell it for £1m in 10 years' time. Achieving both would be a bonus, or half the time you need to do it.

If selling your businesses is the goal, then you need to know how businesses are valued. Accountants will come up with complicated schemes, but the reality is they are sold for a multiple of their annual profits. The profits will be based on the last few years of trading, which is easy to calculate. The multiple is more complicated, as it can depend on many factors, but in general, you can expect to achieve 1-2 times profits for weak businesses that rely too much on the owner and up to 10 times profits for a great business that runs itself. Figures of more than 10 can be achieved but these are rare and often called 'Unicorns', where there is something extra that will enable them to grow massively so their current level of profits are not really the measure – it is all about what they could achieve. Think Uber, Tesla et al.

Back to reality, the average sale value of normal businesses is about 3 times profits, which suggests most businesses are not as great as they could be. My aim with clients is to get their businesses to a value of at least 4-5 times profits, which means that, to sell the business for £1m with a 4 times multiple, you would need to have increased your profits to £250k pa and have the business working without you.

Once we know what this profit figure is, we then have to work out what size of business, in your industry, you need to have built to achieve it. If your net profit is 10%, then you would need £2.5m turnover and probably be employing 25 people. This would then be your aspirational goal. If you want more than £50k per year or to sell the business for more than £1m then you just have to recalculate the numbers.

The number you go for is down to you. It can take just as long to build a £10m business as it does a £1m one. My belief is, as was the case for the short-term goals, aim for something BIG, hairy and audacious, because even if you don't make it, you will do so much better than if you did nothing, or set a small goal and achieved it.

Now, for some of you reading this, goal-setting will be obvious, but for others I imagine your eyes are glazing over, and you may need to re-read this a few times to get your head around these numbers. This is because we are all different, and that leads us on nicely to the next chapter, because, if we want to play the game, we also need to understand what type of player we actually are …

Chapter 3: The Players

I have only been really playing golf for the last 10 years, having got back into it when I was in my 40s. As I explained in my introduction, I started playing when I was 12, but that only lasted for a year or so, when my dad's back injury put a stop to him playing and meant he cancelled our family membership at the golf club. For the next 20+ years, I would only play once or twice a year, when mates had a stag do or birthday bash.

When I finally got back into playing regularly, I must admit, I became rather addicted. What I love about golf is that it suits my personality. I am very competitive, I love learning and self-improvement, and the only thing that really affects my performance is ME!

My new addiction led me to start having lessons with a golf pro, to go to the driving range as often as I could, to get highly irritated about a bad round, and, embarrassingly, to have the odd tantrum! But I gained real enjoyment from seeing my handicap fall from 18 down to single figures, and scoring my first scratch round totally blew me away.

What I found puzzling though was that some of the people I was playing with just didn't have the same outlook on golf as me. I understood that some people just play on the odd occasion, as I did for 20 years, hope to have a nice day out, and not lose too many balls in the process. But I was playing with people who had played every week for many years and still had the same handicap they started out with, and this I just couldn't understand.

These people didn't practice, and they didn't even warm up before playing a round. It was not that they weren't competitive, because they always liked taking money off me when they beat me, but their motivation for playing the game was different to mine, and that intrigued me.

In fact, it was this behaviour in my fellow golfers that inspired me to write this book, because I was seeing exactly the same behaviour in business owners I was meeting through my coaching practice.

I have now coached over 250 business owners and must have met well over 10 times that many in the 15 years I have been coaching. So, I have a large sample from which to draw my conclusions!

Comparing the types of golfers and business owners I have come across, I started to see some real similarities. From analysing these, I could see that they fell into 4 types of players:

1. The Beginner
2. The Improver
3. The Master
4. The Life-styler

I will look at each of these types in turn, and what makes both golfers and businesspeople move between these categories.

The Beginner

All golfers start here; the difference is just that some start early and some start late. It is generally the first few hits of the ball that dictate our future. Those that go on to play a lot of golf will have had a good experience, maybe due to natural ability, or just by a bit of good luck.

If the experience is bad – they miss the ball, lose too many, or play with people at too high a level too soon – they may just give up before they have given it a real go.

The same will be true for people starting their business. The first few months and years can have a major impact on the player's long-term success. If they do get some early wins, such as making that first sale to a customer who buys more and more, achieving a profit in their first year, and taking on a good employee, then this will give them the drive and enthusiasm to push on and potentially build a really great business and achieve their aspirational goals.

On the flip side, if they experience negatives in those first few months and years, such as making losses, running out of cash, or taking on difficult and bad clients and employees, then this can lead them to resenting their business. As a result, they can become reluctant to take on more people, get worried about investing money in marketing or equipment and the business struggles to grow. They never achieve their aspirational goals and often drop out of business altogether.

The really strange thing is that most beginners are normally receptive to help with moving forward. They will dabble with lessons, they may read the odd book, watch a video or two. However, they often feel they are not yet ready for serious lessons.

They want to play the game a little longer before they approach a professional to help them out.

But this of course is crazy. Any golf coach would rather start from scratch with a player and teach them the right things from the beginning, than have to try and fix bad habits that have developed over a period of time. Look around a golf club and most players have bad habits they picked up in the early days. I am forever grateful for those few lessons I had when I was 12 which set me up with some of the basics. I just wish I had been able to continue at that age.

As with golfers starting out with the game, so it is with business owners not getting the help they need to set them up for success in the first few years. In all my 30+ years in business, I have never come across a business owner that has taken actual lessons in how to build a business before they started one.

At best they will have had a number of years running somebody else's business, and if they were lucky that person was very successful and has taught them well. Even entrepreneurs like Sir Richard Branson and Sir Alan Sugar started with no actual knowledge of running a business. They learnt by trial and error and a bit of luck. If you read their biographies they made a lot of mistakes, but because they started young they had time on their side to make it work. They are however the outliers of businesspeople, just like Bubba Watson who, allegedly, has never had a lesson, is an outlier in golf.

The majority of businesspeople start much later in life so have less time to make mistakes. In the first few years, they often rely on family and friends to help and guide them. While this is a cheap way of learning, in many cases it does not help, as these are not professional businesspeople. As a result, bad habits start to form from the start, which inhibit the future growth potential of the business.

Where golf and business differ is that golf is always optional, and your financial safety does not depend on it. If you play and start to dislike it, then you can always stop and do something else. Unfortunately, with business this is unlikely to be the case. Many people in business don't really enjoy all of what they do, but it pays the bills and if not this, then what else could they do? They often feel that they cannot go back to being employed, change what the business does or only do the bit of the role that they do enjoy.

Just imagine how you would feel if you weren't a great golfer and did not really enjoy playing, but you had to play to keep your family alive. I am sure that there are some golf professionals out there that have had this feeling at some time, and I know there are thousands of business owners who feel like this at times.

My recommendation is that all beginners take some lessons as soon as possible. If money and time are limited then do group lessons or fill in the times between seeing your coach with reading books, and watching videos. Practice whenever you can, but make sure you are able to interpret the results by sending videos and results to your coach to give you honest feedback.

Make those early days of learning your game, productive and enjoyable, so that you have the skills you need to move to the next level, as it will be your experiences in these first few months and years that will often dictate which type of player you will eventually become.

The Improver

How long you stay at level 1 really depends on the time you dedicate to "The Game". Some people never get into it fully and will be at the beginner level for a long time. Others will decide it is not the most important thing in their life and become Life-stylers, and for a few they will love the idea of being better and become an improver.

What makes an improver is that they have a real desire to be better and are willing to dedicate the time and money to achieving this. I also believe that there is a certain level of addiction that happens, the great Heavy Metal singer Alice Cooper, once said …

> *"Golf is a far healthier addiction than*
> *others I have had in the past".*

What is really happening with people who are at this level is that their brains are getting natural highs from the four major chemicals that are released and make us feel content and happy. The more they play and practice the more they feel good and so they come back for more. If you don't get these highs or you get higher doses from other things in your life then you are more likely to focus on those activities instead.

These chemicals are Dopamine, Oxytocin, Serotonin and Endorphins, often referred to as "DOSE".

Dopamine makes us feel happy when we are striving or anticipating something good is about to happen. That feeling you had as a kid on Christmas morning, or as that ball is about to drop in the hole. Its purpose is to get us excited about doing something meaningful. Those cavemen who got up in the morning excited about hunting were the ones that found food for their family, those that stayed in bed starved.

Oxytocin is the neurochemical that has allowed us to become social creatures. It makes us feel empathy which helps us feel close and bonded to others when it's released. For the Caveman, it was the fact that they would have a better chance of success hunting together than alone and those that brought food home for their family meant that they would ensure the longevity of their gene pool.

Serotonin is considered a natural mood stabilizer. It's the chemical that helps with sleeping, eating, and digesting. Think of it as the balancer for other chemicals. As it is produced in the gut, a lack of food reduces its production and that's why we can get cranky when we have not eaten. For our cavemen and women it means that when they were hungry they were motivated to hunt, but when they had eaten they were happy to sit and relax.

Endorphins are responsible for masking pain or discomfort and help you "power through." For the caveman this was to ensure they would try harder than their rival and so gain the prize when others gave up too soon.

All of these chemicals are activated during the learning of a particular skill. But only if the goal is exciting enough. Think of our caveman relative, hunting for food. If they were not that bothered then they would not push themselves hard enough to release these chemicals, but when they did the chemicals would help them along the way and reward them when they had secured their goal.

All sports have the power to do this. Think of the runners' high, which is a big hit of endorphins they get to help them keep and push through the pain barrier.

While golf is much less physical than running, the mental game has the same ability to release these chemicals and because it is a social game, you also get the serotonin and oxytocin hits that you don't get from solo pursuits. It also does not matter how you play on the day. When you play well, you get a high because you succeeded. When you play badly, you get a high that says, go practice some more and get better.

Now I am no neural scientist, but I am guessing that there must be a ratio of success to failure, to keep this level of motivation. Too many losses will eventually get you down and mean you will be less likely to go and practice. Too many successes will mean that it becomes too easy, and therefore not as exciting. Although, I am guessing there are very few people out there that ever find golf "too easy"!!

This is the beauty of the game. The handicap system allows anybody to play against anybody else, so you can always compete, have a chance of winning and socialise with others. Also, you are never really playing against other people, you are always playing against the course and yourself. No matter how well you play, you always leave shots on the course, and no matter how badly you play, there is always a good shot in there that brings you back for more.

I hope you can see from this why people like me get addicted to the game of golf. I love watching videos, reading books, getting lessons and putting this into practice. When it works on the course I love playing well, and even when I don't do so well in a round, I become more motivated to practice and try again.

This is the key to the improver level – you have to "feel" like you are improving, even if the scores you are getting do not reflect this.

I look at my game now compared to a year ago and I think it is so much better. Yet, yesterday I shot probably my highest score in 12 months, losing 6 balls (2 on one hole).

The key to enjoying golf, I think, is to remember that there is an element of luck involved, and some days the "golfing gods" are just going to punish you for the hell of it!

If we now look at this Improver level for business people, you should see that everything that I have said for the golf improver also applies to the business improver. In those early years of your business, everything is new and exciting. You are constantly learning, uncovering new things and pushing yourself to a level that you may not have thought possible.

Just like golf there needs to be a good balance between success and failure in business. No successful business person has made it to where they are without a few failures along the way, but these just drive them on. However, I have known business people who seemed to fail too often and lose that motivation and eventually drop out. The difference in my mind is that desire to learn how to be better. If you fail and then try again with no new knowledge or skills then you are likely to fail again. Using that failure to drive you to learn a new and better way is far more likely to lead to success. All the while those neural chemicals are helping you push through and keep you happy.

I have loved working with improvers over the years. I give them a business book, they read or listen to it. Even those clients who have never read a book since they were at school or are dyslexic, start enjoying books when they are relevant to helping them be better. I put on a workshop, and they attend and take copious notes. They listen to podcasts, watch Ted talks, and they just love to learn the skills they need to be better at business. A lost sale motivates them to make the next one. A recession means they pivot and potentially reinvent themselves. While others blame outside influences, make excuses or just deny there is an issue, improvers see failure as a challenge to overcome and look to better themselves to do it.

The brilliant, World Cup winning England Rugby Coach, Sir Clive Woodward, says that there are two types of people, Rocks and Sponges. 'Rocks', you can't teach anything, they know it all or have no desire to learn and better themselves. 'Sponges' on the other hand have a thirst for understanding how to play the game better. And in Sir Clive's words:

*"I cannot work with Rocks, give me
a team of Sponges any day."*

This is why improvers' businesses keep on growing, they just don't stop. Yes, they might have a few setbacks. I have had clients who have built multi-million-pound businesses, only to lose them because of an outside factor that was out of their control, but within a few years they were back, bigger and better than before. Just as I hope I will play better next weekend, after this week's disaster.

I think what defines an improver, is that they live to my formula for life success:

BE x DO = HAVE

Because they want to HAVE more, they are good at setting themselves BIG goals, and setting more goals when they achieve them.

To achieve these bigger goals, they work on their BE, their beliefs, knowledge and skills and they DO more, make plans and take action and put this learning into practice. They will seek out help and support from Mentors and Coaches, to help them get to where they want to go.

As we saw in Chapter 2, the goal is of upmost importance, if it is big and exciting enough, the Improver will be driven to do what ever it takes to achieve it. However, once the goal has been reached or becomes irrelevant then the player must make a choice. Do they sit back and enjoy where they are and become a lifestyle player, or do they push on to become a master…

The Master

The definition of a 'Master' in the context we are talking about is…

"A person who is very skilled in a job or activity."

Demonstration of their mastery is the ease with which they tackle the task in hand. In golf, it is easy to spot these people as they have a scratch handicap, i.e. they are given no shots when they play a course, and they expect to go round in par or better.

In business, the master can be slightly harder to spot, but a good indicator is that they are running a business that to all intents and purposes runs without them, and gives them the lifestyle that that desire. If they continue to work IN the business, it is purely because they love it, and not because they HAVE to.

So the question that arises when you get to this level is, how do you maintain the motivation that got you here in the first place? Well, the answer is simpler than you probably think, and we can look to golf to show it.

Imagine you have worked hard, at the improver level, to finally become a Master at the game. If you have done this at an early enough age, what do you naturally want to do? Become a golf professional, of course. You want to make a career out of playing the game you love. When you start out you are not yet qualified to be called a Master, because you have not won anything of great importance. After all, being considered a Master is in the eyes of others, not your own.

You continue to learn and improve, mastering not only the physical game of golf but also dealing with mental pressure situations where money is at stake, because, after all, this is now your JOB as well as the game you love.

This is where I think it goes wrong for many talented individuals. The added pressure of having to make a living gets in the way of playing the game well and enjoying it. The travel, constant practice, and the knowledge that each mistake can cost you thousands of pounds gets into your head and interferes with the perfect golfer that is inside of you.

But then maybe luck comes into things; you get a good run of results, and sponsors give you money for just wearing their clothes and watches. Your travel is covered, you stay in nicer hotels, fly rather than drive from venue to venue, and so you have more time to practice. You can now easily afford to pay for a coach/caddie.

The pressure to earn money is off, to a certain extent, so you relax a bit. After all, whether you win £100k or £200k this week does not really matter. You just want to win for winning's sake.

Then it all comes together one year, you are playing at the peak of your game. The Masters, or one of the Opens beckons, and you are in with a shout. That day you play the best golf of your life and on Sunday evening, you take home the trophy you have always dreamed of.

So all that practice, the hard work, the constant failure, finally comes good and you are now a Master, right?

Wrong! See, if that were it in sport, the game would not be half as fun for the spectator as it is. Tiger Woods would have only won one Major, Rafa Nadal, Roger Federer and Novak Djokovic would not be pushing their ageing bodies to become the all-time greatest player. Lewis Hamilton and Valentino Rossi would have stopped racing after one world title and enjoyed an easy life of luxury living off their past glory.

What makes a true Master is that they always want more. Recalling a quote from Jim Collins' book *Good to Great*...

"Good is the enemy of Great"

As I said at the start, the game of golf has been around for hundreds, if not thousands of years ,and it will be around for many more. Masters are defined not by achieving one result, but by a life-long pursuit of winning.

After all, why on earth would Tiger Woods come back after 11 years to win his 15th Major, if winning once was enough?

My belief is that Mastery can only come when there is a disconnection between playing the game and earning a living.

It sort of goes full circle – when kids play games, they do so because they just want to play. Likewise, Masters play the game because they just want to play. It is for those in the middle who are having to earn a living where things are not so easy.

So how do we become a Master of business? Well, we must get to a position where money is no longer the main driver for us being in business. As I showed you in Chapter 2 – The Goal, you need to build a business that can work without you, or you can sell. Once you have got to that point, your love for the 'Game of Business' must still be strong enough for you to keep on playing it, and still have a desire to keep on winning.

True Masters are very rare in all walks of life, and in business this is just as much the case. I have been taught by a few, for which I am truly grateful, and I hope I have helped some that will go on to achieve this status within their industries.

In reality, there is no major difference between the improver and the master. Both are determined to be better, continue to learn and seek out people to help them improve. Mastery comes as a result of staying playing the game at the highest level for the love of the game, and not just because you have to, or it pays the bills.

If so few make it to the Mastery level, and we are not cut out to keep working at improving our game, what then of the 4th type of player? Well, I call these the Lifestyle players and you won't be surprised to learn that these account for the largest number of people in golf, business, and in fact all walks of life.

The Life-styler

If you think about the typical golf club with, let's say, 500 members and you were to count the number of members who fell into each of these 4 categories, I would expect less than 1% would be in the Master level (if any), and probably 20% in the Beginner/ Improver levels. This means that 80% of members would fall into the Lifestyler category. So what defines these players?

Players can progress (or regress) into this group from any of the previous 3 groups. Beginners can fall into it, Improvers can decide they no longer want to improve, and even Masters have to take a break. What these players have in common is that the game of golf is not the most important thing in their life. Yes they enjoy the game, but they have found the level that they are comfortable with. The people they play with are at a similar level to them, or their handicap allows them to compete with those players they like to spend time with.

The thought of putting in more effort to be better does not excite them. Those that were Improvers or Masters are content with the level they are at. Those who came straight from being Beginners may feel that lessons would set them back before they would see an improvement.

Some think that lower handicap will make the game harder, or their friends will think of them as being too competitive. Life-stylers get what they need from golf at the level they are, so why should they push for more? This is the beauty of golf, it can be all things to all people, and no one way is the right way. Unfortunately, in the

'Game of Business' the same situation arises, but the outcome is not as pleasant as it is with golf.

When a business person slips into the Life-styler category, they too have reached a level of performance that they are happy with. They are happy working the hours they are working, probably a bit less than they did before. They can pay all the bills at the end of the month and have enough money to pay themselves a reasonable salary and even a dividend at the end of the year, if they have had a good year. This often comes after a number of years of hard graft, risks, and ups and downs, so it is natural to take a deep sigh, sit back and enjoy where they have got to.

Just like the golfer who sits at 18 handicap for the next 10 years, they will socialise with other business people at a similar level, which is fine, but in these situations, the overall purpose of having a business is often forgotten...

"To Build a Commercial Profitable Enterprise that will work without you"

...so that at some time in the future you can be financially free and play as much golf as you like.

As a Business Owner, you have to remember that you are more like a golf professional than a club player, because you have to perform on a daily basis. A bad day can cost you thousands of pounds, and until you have a business that works without you, sold your business or you have saved enough money to be financially free, you must keep on playing the game.

This is why it is so vital to set your goals in business and identify why you are playing the game. If you don't have a clear goal of where you want to be in 5-10 years, then you risk slipping into being a Lifestyle player before it is safe for you to do so.

This is why I believe the best approach is to learn to love learning. If you do this, then you cannot fail to become a better version of yourself, BE more, DO more and HAVE more. You will tap into those happy chemicals in your brain, and even if you never get to be a true Master you will have so much more fun, and never have to look back on your life and think that you could have done better.

The other advantage of continual improvement is that the skills you gain give you confidence to play other courses and businesses, which we explore in the next chapter.

50

Chapter 4: The Course

So far, my golf and business analogy has been easy; the game, goals and players all work nicely in both contexts. I had to think a bit more laterally with the courses we play.

Golf courses are designed to be a challenge, to be different to each other and to push us as players to be better. Players who belong to a club love the fact that the same course they play on week after week, year after year, still proves difficult to master.

Then there is the joy of playing a completely different course, where you cannot rely on your years of experience and must approach the game in a different way.

If golf courses were easy, all the holes the same length and built the same way, I think golf would be extremely dull. It would be more like going to a driving range and hitting balls for the sake of it.

If you think about it, for most sports, the environment in which you play is very static. One dart board is the same as another, squash courts and tennis courts may have slightly different surfaces but are built to a standard size, even football and cricket pitches may have certain quirks, but they are fundamentally the same.

So, why is the key to the enjoyment of golf down to the uniqueness of the courses we play? The key is that in all other sports, which have a standard playing field, the enjoyment is in the competition with your opponent. No way could you play tennis, squash, football or darts against yourself. Even when you practice you would be hard pushed to do this for 4-5 hours in one sitting.

Golf is one of the few sports, (others would be sailing, cross country running, and fishing), where the main competition is the terrain and conditions in which you play the game, and who you are playing against is almost secondary. The reality is that you are just competing against yourself.

It is for this reason that I could quite easily spend a day playing a new course on my own, whereas the thought of throwing darts in a dart board all day for fun, does not do it for me.

With golf, we have a game that is specifically designed to be different and difficult (for more on difficulty, see Chapter 5 on hazards and conditions), and the more difficult it is the more we love it. Yes, we may have the odd tantrum that a bunker is in the wrong place or the pin has been made difficult to get to, but deep down, we would not want it any other way.

In the 'Game of Business' the same is true. The industry in which you work is the equivalent of the type of golf course you play. Some people play the recruitment course, some play the retail course, some the manufacturing course. Just as a golfer will choose the type of golf course they play, be that Links, Forest, or Parkland courses.

The business itself is then like the actual course. Some businesses and courses have been around a long time, while others come and go. St. Andrews has been around since 1754, While Lloyds bank was founded in 1765 and bar a few modifications over the years, both will probably be around for another 250 years! And even if they did disappear, Links golf and banking would survive them.

Just as no two types of golf courses in the same category type are the same, so no two businesses in the same industry will be the same. If you dedicate your life to playing one course/business, then you may well master that course/business, but are you truly a 'Master' if you have never played, let alone mastered many different courses?

This is what I see as a major difference between Masters and Life-styler players. A Master is so confident with playing the game that they revel in a change of course/business. They can take the skills that they have learnt in one and play just as well, sometimes even better, on another.

True business entrepreneurs will have run many different businesses during their careers. Just look at Richard Branson and Alan Sugar. They know that the 'Game of Business' is the same, and they are happy to play on different courses.

If you look at your business in the same way as you look at a golf course, then this should inspire you to want to play the game better and even want to move into other industries, as you would love to play other courses. Also, just because you have not played that course before or it looks intimidating, there should still be an excitement to give it a go. Just think if you got the chance to play at Augusta, would you turn it down, just because you have not played it before?

Business was not designed to be easy, and if you want to enjoy it more, you must accept that and look at it as a game where the fun is in playing as well as you can and always trying to play a little better. Also, you must remember that, like golf, you always have a choice. If you don't enjoy the wind and bunkers on a Links course, you can go and play a Parkland course instead. In business, if you learn how to build a recruitment company but find that it is not floating your boat, take the skills you have learnt and go and choose an industry that does. As long as you have an understanding of how to play the game, it really does not matter which course/business you play.

Unfortunately, as I discussed in Chapter 3, most players are content to stay where they are, in their comfort zone. Even if they don't really like it, they perceive making a change as too difficult, and put up with what they have got.

If that is a conscious decision then great, enjoy what you have but if you have more to give and want to achieve more, then you need to start learning a new way.

There is of course another reason why every player in golf and business needs to keep learning and that is because the conditions in which you are playing will always be changing and one day you will find yourself in a hazard that you have not experienced before...

Chapter 5: The Hazards & Conditions

My home course is Hockley, just outside Winchester on the south coast of England. It is a Downs course, which means it is on the top of a hill, with very little protection from the elements (think inland links course).

The course was built specifically to take into account the normal south-westerly winds, which should be with you on the first 5 holes, against you on the last 5 holes, and with and against you on the other 8.

However, in England the weather changes 'like the wind', and when that wind blows in any other direction, it makes playing the course very interesting indeed.

During the summer, the course dries out like a links course, and the greens become superfast. During the winter, when it has been raining heavily, everything slows up and an extra club or 2 is needed.

Now, this is not unique to our course by any means. Great golf course designers (ours was James Braid) understand that the weather is a key factor in the challenge of golf. They will use the natural hazards, and introduce their own water, contours and bunkers, to bring an element of challenge to the course and make the golfer have to think their way round.

All true golfers appreciate this, and in fact travel long distances and pay high green fees to play on courses that challenge them more. While you will obviously hear the odd swear word when a ball lands in a bunker, disappears into the water or drifts wayward into the trees, deep down the golfer knows that this is just part of the game, and it is the course's way of asking them to try harder and play better.

It therefore does amaze me, having played the 'Game of Business' for as long as I have, that the players don't respond to the hazards in business in the same way.

The weather changes in business, just like it does in golf. One day it is sunny, and it feels like everything is going your way in business. Then you wake up one day, the weather has changed, and everything starts to go wrong.

We need to understand and accept that business macroeconomics runs through seasons, and history shows us that the cycle is about 10 years long. There was the 1970s crash and recovery, the 1980s boom and bust, the 1990-2000 dot com bubble, 2010 financial crash, and now the 2020 Covid crash.

Businesses have summers where everything is bright and cheerful and we can have an easy life. Autumn, or as they say in America, the fall, is when fruits are plentiful, but we all know they cannot last long so we have to work hard to "make hay". It's in winter where things can be a real struggle, and many businesses will not survive. Then we head into spring when new shoots appear, and if we work hard, we can again enjoy the summer months.

In addition to this cycle, every business is going through its own "Rollercoaster ride" (see my first book, *The BIG Dipper* for more on this). Micro economic factors influence businesses all the time, from customers and suppliers, to access to finance and people, to government taxes and industry regulations.

All these factors are outside your control, save the ability to vote for a new government every 4 years, just as the conditions and hazards like wind and the placement of the bunkers are outside the control of the golfer.

Yet I hear so many businesspeople blaming the failure of their business to grow on these "hazards". They say they cannot grow because they cannot find the right people, they run out of cash because they have to pay their taxes, the government have put legislation in place that loses them half of their clients.

But as we all know, "Shit happens!" I learnt this, for the first time, many years ago when, after studying for 5 years for my professional accountancy qualification, I finally qualified, and was greeted by the senior partner with the words:

*"That is great news, well done, but we
cannot now afford to keep you on."*

Then a few years later, the company in which I was Finance Director, and had helped build to £4m in 4 years, lost its main customer and 90% of its business, and had to lay off 49 of its 50 employees.

As they say …

"Failure is one of life's best teachers"

If you read the autobiographies of all the most successful business owners, there is always one key similarity. At some point in their career, they lost or nearly lost everything, and that was a defining moment in their life. At that point, they could have easily given up and gone and got another job. Instead, they decided that their goal was the most important thing in their life, so they buckled down, stopped blaming others, making excuses or just ignoring the problem, they took ownership and said to themselves,

"The only person that can get me through this is me!"

Just as a golfer, in fact me yesterday, after failing to score on 4 out of the first 5 holes, gets themselves back in the game, so failures and set backs are just temporary inconveniences for the business person who has a clear goal of the business they are building

Golf is a funny game, and the same is true about business. It is not biased, it does not remember, it does not hold grudges and there is always an element of luck involved. But, as the great Gary Player is quoted as saying…

"The more I practice the luckier I get!"

I think that that is one of the biggest lessons we can learn when playing the 'Game of Business'. The challenges you are going to face are just part of the game. Yes, they can be frustrating but this should inspire you to be better. Jim Rohn's quote sums this up perfectly.

*"Never wish your life were easier,
wish that you were better"*

If you start to think of challenges as a test to see how important the goal you are working towards is, then you will be on the right track.

If you want to shoot par on a hole and you end up in a bunker then you will need to have great bunker skills to save your par. If you need more people to do the work you have, then you need to have great recruitment skills.

Just swearing at the bunkers or lack of people is useless. The danger is that if you don't learn these skills and you are not really bothered about your goals then you will dumb your goals down to the level of your current competence.

Now go back and re-read Chapter 2 – the Goal. And if you did not do it the first time, work out the ultimate goal of your business. How much do you want to sell it for, or have it earn for you when you are not HAVING to work in it?

If you really want this goal, then no matter what hazard you come across or what the weather throws at you, you will do what is necessary to overcome it. You may have to decide to change your player status from Life-styler to improver, but I know from having coached hundreds of businesspeople, there is more fun in moving forward and learning to play the game better than there is in standing still and moaning about things outside your control.

So, where do you start when wanting to play the game better? Well, why not start to learn how to use the tools of the trade, the clubs…

Chapter 6: The Clubs

When I first played golf as a kid, my dad took me to the practice area, gave me a pitching wedge and I happily swung away at the ball for an afternoon, having a great time.

At the time, I had no idea that there were another 13 clubs that I could use. In fact, I was so bad at hitting with the one I had, the thought of using any others probably scared me to death.

Then after a few weeks of steady improvement, I got interested in the other clubs in the bag. The putter was the next one, as it was a completely different club and was actually easier to use. Then as every kid does, I saw the woods (they were woods when I started, half the size of the drivers today, but equally as sexy). Oh boy! Did I want to hit that ball as far as I could, but oh boy, was it virtually impossible for me.

Then there was that 3 iron. After one hit, I realised that it was not for me, and I don't think I hit with one again for 30 years, so painful was the first experience.

Therein lies the beauty of golf. I think that it is the only sport where you must master 14 different pieces of equipment. Even in other hobbies, such as playing musical instruments, while the skills you learn with one instrument allow you to play another, it would take you a long time to master 14, and then play them all perfectly in one 4 hour session. If golfers were musicians, we would be playing every instrument in the orchestra. Imagine the noise!!

What crazy mind decided that they would put in a bag 14 different tools to do essentially the same thing, and not only that, but make some big, some small, some short, some long and some designed for only one thing.

Since I got back into golf in my 40s, I have really enjoyed learning how to master each club. There are days where I can drive like a demon, but my short game deserts me. There are days when I can hit 90% of greens in regulation (i.e. 1 shot par 3, 2 shots par 4, 3 shots par 5), but then go on to hit 3 or 4 putts and ruin a great score.

Just like in the orchestra, I may have 90% of the instruments working well, but the ones that are out of tune or sync destroy the whole performance.

Even golf professionals who play the best round of their career will look back and feel that there were one or two shots that were not quite there and cost them the perfect round.

Every elite athlete works towards perfection, but knows that they may only achieve it once or twice in their lifetime. Yet it is the pursuit of perfection that keeps them coming back. The perfect qualifying lap in F1, the total clearance in snooker, or the 9 dart finish.

In business, instead of using clubs to play the game, we use strategies. Just like golf, you could play the game using only one, but you would never master the game, nor would you achieve as much success as somebody playing the same game who has mastered more than one.

So, what are these strategies, and do the similarities to golf extend further? Well, if we use a bit of poetic licence, I think that they do.

Just as golf clubs can be broken down into 4 types, woods, irons, wedges, and putters, so business can be broken down into 4 areas:

1. Finance & Administration,
2. Sales & Marketing,
3. Operations and
4. People.

To master the 'Game of Business' we have to master each of these areas.

Everybody who starts or buys a business that lasts at least 12 months will have skills in at least one of these areas.

My father, who was an accountant, was great in Finance and Admin. He bought an established business and thought that he could run it as well as the previous owner, because of his skills in this area.

However, he knew nothing about sales and marketing, and was not great at people management. While he learnt a lot about the operational side of the business from the previous owner, he did nothing about improving his skills in these other areas, which meant that the business stopped growing and eventually, after 15 years, ceased trading because of the change in the economic climate in the early 1990s.

I have seen brilliant sales people start businesses, but quickly run out of cash because they did not understand how the numbers worked, and overlooked the fact that…

*"Turnover is vanity, Profit is sanity but
Cash is King"*

Technicians such as plumbers, electricians, even accountants and lawyers, are brilliant at the operational side of things. But in many cases, they are so good at this that they forget that they should be building a business that works without them, and fail to build a team of people better than they are to run their business for them.

In golf, this would be like being a brilliant putter but always losing the ball off the tee. You have to be great at all 4 areas to build a great business and be a great golfer.

Now, I don't have time in this book to give you any strategies in these 4 areas of business, because there are so many. In my 2nd book, *Profit Builders*, I identify 11 of the most important ones to create profit. But take it from me, it is like having an infinite bag of clubs, and the challenge with having too much choice is that you can often just stick to what you have always done.

I call this the "Indian Restaurant syndrome." You have 10 pages to choose from on the menu, so what do you do? Order Chicken Tikka Masala, the same as always!

With golf, I have loved learning how to play each club properly. I even stuck a 2 iron in the bag, and no longer have the childhood fear of my 3 iron.

For each club, you need a lesson in how to play it well, as there are infinite shots you can play with each club. In business, each area has multiple strategies that you are continually learning how to master and I believe that the beauty of both games is that there is an infinite need to learn and relearn as you continue to play the game, and conditions change.

The final point in this chapter is that once you have mastered your set of clubs, you feel far more comfortable playing other courses in any condition. So too, once you have mastered strategies in the 4 areas of business, you will feel confident about playing other games of business. This is why master entrepreneurs like Richard Branson and Alan Sugar don't worry about the business they are playing. They rely on their knowledge in each of these areas to be able to play the game as well as anybody else.

However, before you play another course or another business it is a good idea to know one final thing, the rules of the game....

Chapter 7: The Rules

Every game you play has a set of rules, which were set out when the game was first invented. These rules let you know what you can and can't do, and thereby ensure that the game is played as fairly as possible. Without rules, arguments will arise, and the game will take a sour turn. If you have ever played a game where two people disagree on a rule, then you will understand where I am coming from.

Over the years, the rules can be added to or adapted as the game develops. Just look what happened in 2020 to the rules in golf - many rules were changed or added, to try and speed up the game, as the modern world is moving at a quicker pace, and we no longer have 5 hours to invest in the game, if we ever truly did.

It is always the players' responsibility to learn the rules, and in social golf, more experienced players help the newbies, and those that try to bend the rules should be picked up by their playing partners. In professional matches there are referees wandering the course, with the rule book in their pocket, hoping for an incident that puts their knowledge to the test.

Breaking the rules leads to punishment, shot strokes and even disqualification, but it is the stigma of cheating that really keeps players in check. Although I have played with one or two people over the years who don't seem to care, and are prepared to take the risk.

In all cases the rules are not designed to make the game easier, only to make it clearer and ensure everybody is treated equally and there is no ambiguity. Just like I said in Chapter 5 - The Hazards and Conditions, they are not personal and are out of your control. So why do we often feel that, when they work against us, (e.g. mud on the ball, hitting it out of bounds) that they were written solely for the purpose of making us feel bad and ruining our score.

However, we all know that the game would not be what it is without the rules of the game. In business the same is true, but with a slight twist.

In business, there are actually very few rules. Most of the rules that do exist are part of the business economic environment you are playing in, e.g. the amount of tax you pay, the records you have to keep; how you advertise and what you can sell to whom.

Apart from that, how you play the game is 100% down to you, so in effect you get to write the rule book.

Now, if you only ever intend to play the game on your own or with your best mate, you probably don't need to write anything down. You can score as you like, move the ball if it is behind a tree and take as many "mulligans" as you wish.

But if you intend to play the game with and against others, you need to all play by the same rules.

The business rule book comes in many forms, but is essentially the systems and processes of your business. To see these in action, you have to look at some of the best and most successful businesses in existence. My favourite for demonstrating this is McDonald's restaurants.

The McDonald's empire started out in 1948 as a small burger bar in California run by two brothers, who had a great system to produce a great quality burger at an affordable price and to serve lots of them very quickly. However, they had no desire (goal) to build a business beyond this. It would be like seeing a golfer who can shoot 10 under par every time they play, but who says,

"Nah, I am happy playing my home course,
I don't want to become a professional"

Then in 1954, along came Ray Croc, a washed up, 50-year-old milkshake machine salesman. He saw the potential in the McDonald brothers' business model and opened a restaurant in Illinois. From there, he went on to build the world's largest restaurant chain.

The reason he could do this was three-fold:

1. He wanted to, it was his goal
2. He knew about the 4 areas of business I referred to in Chapter 6
3. He systemised everything and created a rule book so anybody could play.

A typical McDonald's restaurant has annual sales of about £2.5m and makes a profit of around £250K+. It is run by managers whose average age is approximately 24, and staffed by 18-year-olds who only stay in the job for about 9 months. Oh, and once the restaurant is set up and running, the owner only needs to pop in a few times a year to make sure all is well.

So how does a business of this size work as efficiently as it does? The answer is simple – SYSTEMS!!

Your systems are your "rule book", they show the players of the game how to play. The number of systems/rules will depend on the competency of the players and the complexity of the game.

Making burgers is quite a simple process, but the players are young and don't have a lot of skill, so the systems need to be very robust. Within your business, you have to decide what level your systems are, and a good indication is always how consistent the results are, and how many problems you need to fix on a day to day basis.

In my coaching experience, one of the biggest frustrations of business leaders is that their teams are not performing as well as they want. They say…

"if only I could get good people!"

Well, the answer I give is that you get the people you deserve. If your team are not performing, you need to look at yourself first, your systems second and the team last.

So where do you start with writing the rule book for your business? Well, follow the same method that you would if you had just created a new game or sport.

First, you would want to write down the purpose of the game, and how you are going to know what winning looks like, i.e. WHY are we here? (See Chapters 1 & 2 - The Game & The Goal). If you would like further reading on this, then I can recommend Simon Sinek's book, *Start with Why.*

After this, I would recommend you write down the core values of your business. These will be the guiding principles that you work by, and that you would expect everybody coming into your business to work to. There may only be 3 -6 real core values. These are expressed either as a noun, such as Passion and Knowledge, or a short phrase, such as Work Hard and Be Kind.

One thing you should avoid is putting these values into a context, i.e. passionate about our clients. This is because true values are used in any situation - even the way you make a cup of tea!

Next, you need to set the scene for where your business is heading, i.e. your vision of the future, and finally you need a plan of how you are going to get there.

The equivalent in golf would be planning your match-winning round. Which holes are you going for birdie, and on which will you accept a bogey. Of course, when the first ball is hit the plan is likely to change, but by having visualised as many situations you could come up against, you will be in a better position mentally to cope, even if it is something you have not encountered before.

In business, you should have your rules and systems for each of the 4 areas mentioned in Chapter 6 - The Clubs.

Finance and Admin: systems are how you record and report the data, and how you control the cash in and out. Established businesses will rely on computer programmes to carry out much of these operations, so the systems can come from those user manuals, but your data entry and reporting is likely to be unique to you.

Sales and Marketing: in this area, systems are often overlooked, but are key to success. Again, computer software such as Client Relationship Management (CRM) Systems can help with this. Brand guides give marketers the rules on how they promote your business, while sales processes should be documented to achieve consistently great results.

Operations: this is the area that probably does get the attention it deserves, with Lean Processes and ISO standards giving frameworks on which to build your systems. Just make sure that for those of you who are the technicians who do the work, you spend time documenting how you like things done, so that others who might not be as good as you can still do a good job.

The People: this side of things is often ignored in smaller businesses, and not given the attention it deserves in larger ones. There should be clear recruitment, induction, disciplinary and motivation systems. Organisation charts, roles and responsibilities and meeting schedules should all be in place if you really do care about keeping your team motivated.

The more complex your business, the more systems and processes you need, but the benefit will be huge, as new recruits will be up to speed quicker. Team members who do not follow the rules can be brought to account. But the biggest benefit is that, if you know your systems and they are written down and shared across your organisation, you can then work on improving them little by little. Once you have your systems in place, you break your organisation down into smaller parts, improve each one, then put it back together to get an amazing difference. If you

want to see this in action look at the 5 ways video on my website –
www.abc-solent.co.uk

This concept of Marginal Gains in sport is well known, from the British cycling team, English Rugby squad and yes, even in golf. Look what Bryson DeChambeau has done to his game in 2020.

Systemising your business will also allow you to keep track of your numbers so much better. In all sports, and especially golf, if you can't keep the score, you can't play the game…

Chapter 8: The Score Card

We all have a love hate relationship with our score card. When the numbers are good, it is the best thing ever. I have even kept my card for my first ever scratch round. But when we have a bad day the score card goes straight in the bin. We may even get fed up halfway round and give up keeping score.

But every round we play, we are starting with a clean card and know that it is only ever a reflection of past activity and not future results. We also know that without keeping score the game is just not the same.

There are also different games of golf we can play, Medal (total number of shots), Stableford (points for how you score each hole), Matchplay (win or lose a hole), and you have to be sure which game you are playing, and score appropriately.

Obviously, you can cheat, or make up a better score than you really have, but you are only cheating yourself, so where is the fun in that.

Everybody who is playing the game with you knows the score. When you get to play team golf, such as in the Ryder and Solheim Cup, every member of the team must be aware of how they are doing, and how the team is doing.

Nobody in any sport hides the score from the players. Nobody forces them to keep score. In every sport and game you play, the players want to know and take ownership of their score, and do what they can to help the team to win.

So then, what the hell is happening in business? If you agree with me that business is just a game, then why do so few players really understand how their game is being scored, let alone what the actual score is right now?

Having spent many years in accountancy, I was lucky to have been trained in how to score businesses. But looking back on those days, I realise that often I was not helping the businesses I was doing the accounts of, because I was giving them their score 3-9 months after they had finished that year's game.

This would be like a professional golfer completing the Masters in April and being told their score and where they finished on Christmas Day!

Every game you play and enjoy requires instant feedback for you to know if you are playing it well. This allows you to adapt your game play accordingly. I admit that sometimes this can be counterproductive. Going down the 18th knowing that you have just had 17 of the best holes of your life and a par here will set a new personal best can put on a bit too much pressure, but the professionals learn how to deal with this.

We saw in the first two chapters that Profit is the overall goal for a business. Most business owners will have knowledge of their annual profit/loss, at least on an annual basis, and with modern accounting software it has certainly made this easier than the days of paper records and extended trial balances, allowing the majority of businesses can get access to their figures at least once a month.

However, even this is too slow if you want to play the game to win. Business is a game that is played on a day-to-day basis and your players (team) need to know each day,

"did I win my Game of Business today?"

As we learnt in earlier chapters, just like golf, business is a multifaceted game and if we want to play it better, we must break it down into its component parts.

In Chapter 6 we broke golf down into 4 areas, woods, irons, wedges and putting. So, if I was a golfer looking to improve my game I would want to know my score, not just overall, but for each of these areas.

How many fairways did I hit?

How many greens in regulation?

My up and downs?

How many putts per round?

As the science and data capture techniques in golf have improved, the information and numbers at our disposal have grown. Launch monitors record everything - spin, smash factors, speed and angles. Add to this, body monitors and video techniques, and the data which the player and their coach have to help improve each area of their game allows them to get real time feedback and allow incremental improvements. This means that we can keep pushing what is possible within the game.

This is what Masters of their game do. As we saw in Chapter 3 - The Players, Masters and Improvers love to improve, so they will happily spend time analysing data and reviewing video to gain that 1% improvement in an area. They know if they can do this 10 times, they will get a 10% improvement and 50 times will give them + 50%.

So why is it that I rarely see this level of commitment to the numbers in business? Well the answer is clear in Chapter 3. Just as most golfers are Life-stylers, so too are most business people.

For this reason, there is no interest in the numbers that could help them improve. As long as there is cash in the bank then what the heck, going into that much detail seems too much like hard work.

But for those that want to improve, what numbers in businesses are as important as those in golf? The answer is, the same process applies. What gets measured gets improved, so first decide what area you want to get better at, then find the measurements that can demonstrate the improvements:

Financial numbers are about profit and cash.

Sales and marketing measurements are number of leads, conversion rates, average sales value and number of transactions.

Operations measures are about efficiencies, delivery times and quality.

People is about measuring happiness, retention and motivation.

Just like golf, the technology that is available to help with this data is amazing. CRM systems can track leads and conversion rates. Google analytics has more data than any human can absorb. Enterprise and Manufacturing Requisite Planning (ERP & MRP) systems will show the efficiency and profitability of every job you do, while HR systems keep track of the people side of things.

Today, there is no excuse for "I can't measure that," and if you can measure it, you can improve it. If you want your team to play the game to the best of their ability, you have to arm them with the numbers they need and support them to improve and play better tomorrow. Which brings us on nicely to your team...

Chapter 9: The Team

My golfing analogy runs a bit thin in this section, because golf is not really a team sport. However, if we consider the Ryder and Solheim Cups, where it does become a team game, then I think we can make a go of it. If you struggle with this, then just think of football, rugby or any other sport where it is a pure team game.

Most businesses start out as a solo game. The founder kicks it off, proves the model and then somewhere down the line, realises that they need help. They start by employing their family and friends. This works well to start with, but often leads to problems, firstly because they rarely have all the skills that the roles allocated to them require, and secondly because it is very difficult to fire them if they are not performing!

I suppose this could be like the young golfer having their overkeen parents coach them. While in rare cases the parents do a great job, (think Tiger Woods and the Williams sisters in tennis,) in most cases, such situations lead to fallings out and resentment. I know from first-hand experience, as I really did not get on working with my father and went away to make my own career rather than working with him.

The next mistake that business owners make is hiring somebody quickly to fill a gap. Often the new entrepreneur achieves some early success. They are obviously good at what they do, and the customers start coming on board. As a result, they get very busy and suddenly need an extra pair of hands to help them out. To be honest, at this stage, any pair of hands will do. If there are no friends or family members available to help, then the advert goes out, and the first person who looks like they have the skill gets the job.

This starts off well, as the new recruit has the skills needed, but there is just something about them that does not fit with the culture and values of the founder. It is normally little things that start to irk at first. The way they treat the customer, finish the job, or complete the paperwork, is just not how the founder likes it to be done. But they are too busy to deal with it, and often too scared of confrontation to call them on it, and if they did, what if they left? There is just too much work to risk it. So, they let it go, once, twice, often many times. I have worked with some clients who have done this for many years, and if they do something about it now, they have the added issue of a large redundancy payment or claim for unfair dismissal.

This is why the rules of the game and systems are so important. However, the main damage of not dealing with team members who do not live to the rules of your game is the effect they have on the other team members who do.

Just imagine you are a great team member, working really hard and following the rules, and one of your teammates is not. They are bending the rules, taking short cuts, and as for their attitude, well, frankly, it stinks. Yet the boss does nothing about it, doesn't say one word. It gets worse, because if you do something out of line, you get picked up on it right away, but this guy! He seems to have a Teflon coat.

This eventually leads to one of two behaviours from this good team member, both of which will impact on business performance. Either they start giving up and following in the bad performer's footsteps. Or they leave and go and find a new team, where this poor behaviour is not tolerated.

"The bad apple will always rot the barrel"

Now, I said at the start of this chapter the analogy is a bit thin in golf as it is not really a team game, and when it is, what we see is the pinnacle of performance, so they rarely make these basic errors. But I know you will have seen examples many times in other sports.

The best team captains or managers pick their squads not only on talent, but on how they will integrate as a team. Ian Poulter is regularly called into the Ryder Cup squad, even when he has not been on form, because he is an amazing team player and his commitment to the team is 100%.

On the other hand, Tiger Woods has regularly struggled in the team format, because he has worked on his solo composure for so long. When you see him in a team play environment, he looks uncomfortable with the pressure of his team on his back. But you would have to be a very tough and focused captain not to include him in your squad.

Looking further afield, Sir Clive Woodward is a great example of a manager who picked his squad on attitude and trained them for the skills that he needed. He was also ruthless on those that saw themselves bigger as an individual than the team itself. His book *'Winning'* is a great read on how to build a winning culture in your team.

The mistake that you need to avoid when building your team is to think that it is easy and will happen by itself. If your goal is to build a commercial profitable enterprise that works without you, then you HAVE to build a great team to run it.

Building a team takes time, effort and money, and you have to learn to be a great leader in order to achieve it. Going back to my four areas of business, in my mind the "People" area is the equivalent of putting in golf. You have to keep working at it, and no matter how good you think you are, there will be days when it never seems to work. But there are also days when you can't miss! It will always be possible to improve if you work at it, and work at it you must, because of all the 4 areas, this is the greatest barrier to business growth.

Finance and admin can always be outsourced, and sales could come in even if you are rubbish at marketing. If you deliver an adequate product or service, as long as there is no real competition, you can make money. But try growing a bigger team when you are not great at it, and it will always trip you up.

I think this is the main reason why so many businesses become lifestyle businesses. In fact, I carried out a review of the number of companies in the UK who employ less than 10 people, as a percentage of all the companies in the UK.

The result was – hold onto your hat – a staggering 98%. This means that only 2% of businesses manage to grow big enough to run without the business owner, not because the business can't grow, but because the owner does not have the skill or desire to do it.

If you have ever thought, "It was so much easier when I only had a few team members," then you are likely to be one of these people. As I said at the beginning, if this is a positive choice you've made, then great, but if it is just an excuse then you still have time to do something about it.

You just need to understand how to think like a winner…

Chapter 10: The Mind

The best and most challenging aspect of golf is that it is more than just a physical game. High energy sports such as rugby, football and motor racing rely on a heightened state of physical performance, and a large percentage of the game is played in this state. But in golf, you spend more time not hitting the ball than you do actually hitting it.

It takes, on average, 1 minute 12 seconds to address and hit the ball, therefore, hitting par on a par-72 course extrapolates to exactly 100 minutes, or 1 hour and 40 minutes. This begs the question, what are you doing for the other 3 hours 20 minutes?

In his brilliant book, *'The Inner Game of Golf'* Timothy Gallwey identifies that, in all sports, there are two games being played. The outer game - the physical technique of hitting the ball, and the inner game – the mental gymnastics that are undertaken in the time you are not actually hitting the ball.

I share his view that it is the inner game which is the biggest factor that dictates success or failure in all games. Our thoughts have far more impact on our game than our grip, swing or even the weather, hazards or opponent.

Take that time when you were having a good round and hitting the ball well. There seemed to be an ease with which you swung the club, the ball strike was pure, and the ball landed where you wanted it to. Then you arrive at your bogey hole, the one you hate and has been a card wrecker in the past. The water is there beckoning your ball, the bunkers are in the wrong place for your drive, or there's that tree that always seems to be in the way.

You realise that you are on for a winning score today if you can just get through this hole with a par or bogey. So you play safe, tense up, and hit the ball exactly where you were trying to avoid hitting it.

"Why did I do that!" you scream in your head. "I should have just gone for it as I have on every other hole".

It has nothing to do with your outer game, your grip, stance, takeback or follow through. It is all to do with the inner game, your thought process, and the effect that it has on your outer game.

You have to remember that the human species has been evolving for millions of years. While other species have grown long necks to reach tall branches, long noses to hunt for food, or radar to fly by, we have evolved our brains to make us the most dominant species on the planet (some would say too dominant, but it will be our brains that will solve this problem). However, much of our thinking is not a lot different from our Chimpanzee cousins.

If we want to know how to play the inner game as well as the outer game, we need to start by understanding how our brains have evolved and work.

All animals are wired to react to external stimulus. When one of our 5 senses, hearing, seeing, smelling, tasting or touching are exposed to an external stimulus, our brain engages, and has to assess what is happening. This function is carried out by our Reticular Activating System (RAS), whose job it is to send the information to the right part of the brain.

There are 3 parts to the brain that have evolved over the millennia. The first and oldest is:

The reptilian brain – We share this with all animals, and it is there to keep us and our species alive. It controls our muscles, heart, breathing and other bodily functions. It dishes out adrenaline to heighten our senses and muscle reactions when we are in danger so that we can fight, flee or freeze. It is ultra-quick, short term, and is good at remembering danger and bad things, so that you can avoid them in the future.

To see this in action just look at a crocodile, unchanged in its evolution for millions of years. It survives brilliantly, but you could not say it is a social or intelligent animal. This is because it lacks the next level of brain development:

The limbic system (or mammalian brain) – We share this with higher level social mammals. Because we have evolved as a pack animal, we survive better in groups than on our own. The mammalian brain deals with the complexities of working in groups and fitting in with the herd. Use of this part of the brain is often called emotional intelligence, whereby we learn to understand our own emotions and those of the people around us. This is where our feelings come from – love, happiness, sadness.

While not as instantly active as the reptilian brain, the limbic system is still quick to give us "feel good" hormones such as serotonin, oxytocin and dopamine that we covered in Chapter 3. These are our natural highs, and they are especially good at getting us to repeat the behaviour that causes them.

To see this part of the brain in action, look to the higher-level primates, gorillas and chimps, in their social groups. They seem to have a lot more fun than the crocodile.

However, it is the third and youngest part of our brain that sets humans apart from all other animals:

The neocortex - this is our human or thinking brain. While the reptilian brain is almost fully formed when we are born, and the limbic system quickly develops in our early years, the neocortex takes more time to develop. It grows through learning, and continues to do so as long as we continue to use it. Because of this, and the fact that it is the furthest from the Reticular Activating System, it is the slowest to react and respond. It is the part of our brain that is aware of itself and makes us human. This is what Descartes alludes to in his famous quote:

"I think, therefore I am"

This shows some of its power. But it is far more than this.

The limbic system and reptilian brain work in the now, i.e. they live in the moment, react to what is happening right in front of you. Think of a child who has just fallen over. Their limbic system feels pain, and instantly causes them to cry to gain attention from their parents. There is no "thinking", it just reacts.

The neocortex, on the other hand, can live in the future, past and present. It has the ability to learn from things that have happened, help us deal with complex puzzles in the now and project itself into the future. It is where our ideas come from. Everything that humans have created comes from this part of the brain.

When all three parts of the brain work in unison great things happen. We think, feel and act in extraordinary ways.

Many call this state, "being in the Zone", and it has almost mythical status, especially in sports. It leads to the perfect F1 lap, the perfect shot in golf, the perfect ace in tennis.

However, as we all know, this state is often hard to come by, let alone maintain, so we must keep reminding ourselves that it is actually our natural state. We do not need to search for it, we just have to ensure things don't get in the way of it happening. But this is harder than it would seem, especially when these 3 parts to our brain can work against each other, and create problems that are not actually there.

In his international best seller, 'The Chimp Paradox', Professor Steve Peters refers to the limbic system as our chimp brain, and explains that it is there to protect us from feeling bad. But, like a chimp, if things are not going its way, it gets angry, beats its chest and throws its toys out of the pram.

The reptilian brain is there to keep us alive, but it does not know the difference between a real threat and one that is imagined. So, if we think something bad could happen, the reptilian brain will take control, fill us full of adrenaline, and off we go like an antelope running from a lion.

The neocortex can trip us up, because of its ability to project into the future. It can start to create dangers and problems that are not actually there. All phobias come from the neocortex imagining a dangerous situation, causing our limbic system and reptilian brains to kick in, and making those tiny spiders seem like monsters.

So, all those bad decisions you make on a golf course, the putt that you pull left, the drive that you tell yourself not to hit hard but then whack the skin off it, are all because your 3 brains are working against themselves. What you must learn to do is to get your 3 brains to work together, and you do this by practising.

Your training sessions are where you develop the mental game to perform at a high level. Here your neocortex can think, analyse and learn. Your limbic system can start to feel what is a good shot and a bad shot, and your reptilian brain figures out how to move the muscles in your body in the right order and timing to hit that little white ball where you want it to go.

Then, when you get out on the course you should only use your neocortex to analyse the conditions, think ahead and plan the shot. After that, you must switch it off and allow the reptilian brain to execute the shot and the limbic system to fill you with endorphins when you sink that par for a birdie. After a brief moment of enjoyment, your neocortex needs to kick in again, before the next shot, to calm everything down, so that you don't go and smash the very next shot out of bounds.

Hopefully, you can see that how you think can affect your performance on the golf course as much, if not more than, any physical technique that you have. This is the reason why some brilliantly talented golfers never make it as professionals. While they have the skill to hit a ball as well as anybody, the way they think and react holds them back.

The key is to get your neocortex engaged, because this part of the brain is where the ideas and problem solving comes from, but for it to work well you must give it time to think.

Sir Clive Woodward refers to high pressure moments in rugby as T-CUP moments where you have to:

"Think Correctly Under Pressure."

He would constantly train his team for these moments, and this resulted in them winning the World Cup in 2003.

One of the best visible examples of this was Jonny Wilkinson's conversion kicking. When you see him preparing for a field goal, you can see he is giving himself time to engage his neocortex. He controls his breathing and focuses on the outcome he is wanting by visualising the ball sailing through the posts. But once he has set the goal and visualised the outcome, he allows his reptilian brain to take over and do the thing that he has been training relentlessly for.

In business the same is true, although business is even more of a mental game than it is a physical one. This is one of the reasons why age is no limitation to being in business. Ray Croc, the founder of McDonald's, was well in his 50s when he started the company, and Warren Buffet is still playing in his 90s.

I also believe that this mental game is the main reason why businesses struggle to grow, and why too few business owners actually achieve the financial freedom that I talked about in Chapter 1.

Running a business in its early stages is a struggle. The owner has to put all their money into it, plus loads of time and effort. Often there is not enough money to pay the bills, and the owner's thoughts are "if this does not work, I am done for".

As a result of this negative thinking, their reptilian brain kicks in. They are in "Fight or Flight" mode, adrenaline levels are high, the focus becomes short term and they do more physical work, rather than spend more time thinking.

So, the plumber fixes more taps, the accountant does more tax returns and the dentist drills more teeth. While this activity serves them well in the short term, it means they have a business that is not really a business, it's just a JOB. I have lost count of the number of business people that have told me they are too busy to spend an hour talking to me, even when they know deep down that they need some help.

Some business owners do get beyond this stage and start to engage their limbic system by aiming for goals that make them feel good, such as making more money, employing a team around them, and even having more time to do the things that they want to. But even then, the limbic system can trip them up.

They start to feel unloved by their staff, or customers, who take advantage of their good nature. Team members leave or misbehave or they just start to lose love for the business they have been in for a number of years.

Then, even their neocortex can trip them up as it starts to visualise an uncertain future or one where things go wrong. Every opportunity comes with risk that might cost them.

Suddenly, these thoughts and feelings wake up the reptilian brain. Even though the business owner is far from being in a bad place, the reptilian brain kicks in and begins the fight, flight or freeze actions.

Imagine the situation where the reptilian brain feels under threat but can't decide whether to fight or run away, the limbic system feels lonely and ignored, and the neocortex has 101 ideas and possibilities to consider, but it is constantly bombarded by outside factors, such as family, team members, clients and the economy. It is not surprising therefore that mental health issues are common in people who own and run businesses.

Many books have been written about the use of meditation and mindfulness as techniques to help quieten the noise that we all experience in stressful situations. My favourite comes from 'The Inner Game' books by Timothy Gallwey, where he uses a great formula:

$$Performance = Potential - Interference$$

I love the simplicity of this. If you want a high level of performance, you have to increase your potential and reduce the interference.

It is relatively easy to increase your potential. You just need to learn more, and practice more.

Reducing interference is more difficult, because on the surface there are two types, internal and external. Internal interference comes from our inner thinking as I have described above. External interference comes from the world around you. In business, this is from your customers, team, suppliers, the bank, the economy.

In golf, this is from the wind, the course, and even your playing partners. But if you relate this back to what I have said before, these external factors are only interfering with you because you THINK they are. This means then that all interference (bar a punch in the face) is internally driven. So how the hell do you deal with this?

The answer is that you first have to be aware that you have interference, and that it is negatively impacting on you. Many people in life are oblivious to their mental health, or they think it is just the way they are. Only in the last decade or so have we started to take this seriously. Autism and dementia are forms of mental interference caused by physical conditions in the brain. Stress, anxiety and depression have a similar effect, but are mostly mentally created. We are still not 100% sure how to deal with these conditions. Drugs are a way, but to me they are just easing the symptoms, not sorting the underlying problem.

It goes without saying that if you have serious mental health issues, then you do need to seek professional help. But most of us just have a little bit of interference which is not life threatening, so it's easier just to ignore it. But if we do ignore it, we are not dealing with it, and thus our performance will suffer.

I believe that the cause of interference comes from the neocortex. It gets stuck trying to solve unsolvable problems, like a computer in a loop. Because it is so good at reflecting on the past, dealing with what is in front of it and visualising about the future, all this information gets it tied up in a knot.

When it does this, sleep patterns are affected. Sleep is the brain's way of resetting, and thus if we don't get enough sleep, our minds don't reset and we get less and less able to solve the problems we are experiencing. The phrase, "let's sleep on it" shows that we need the mind to settle to solve complex issues.

Self-awareness must therefore start with you asking yourself a few simple questions:

1. Am I sleeping well? Try using a sleep App if you are not sure. There is a difference in the types of sleep. Just lying in bed looking at the ceiling is not sleep.
2. How am I feeling right now? Am I anxious, stressed, happy, sad? Keep a log of your feelings, and look for patterns.
3. Do I feel I have the ability to change my state of mind? The answer should always be yes, but if you say no then it just means you do not have a method to do so just yet.

In most cases, when you ask these questions of yourself, you will break the loop and feel in control again. Breathing deeply and smiling will also help, as they calm the reptilian and limbic systems (after all, you are not actually being attacked by a savage animal). Meditation and Mindfulness are useful techniques in this situation. But, if you ask the questions and don't know how to change, then you are going to need some external help. Having somebody to talk to is the biggest factor in overcoming mental interference.

"A problem shared is a problem halved"

The person you talk to should not be somebody associated with the problems you are trying to solve. You need an external and impartial person to listen to what you have to say and provide unbiased feedback. Talking to friends and family can work, but be careful – because they are close to you, they may not be impartial enough to really help you through your problems. If it is general mental health you need help with, then professional therapists and counsellors are the way to go.

In business, if you are the boss, you obviously can't talk to your subordinates about how you feel. It might feel odd to talk to your colleagues or peers, and family will not be impartial, as they will always see things from your perspective.

To get a truly impartial external sounding board, you should use professional business and executive coaches, because they understand how the 'Game of Business' is played. In golf, and in sport generally, the serious players have caddies and coaches to call upon, and often will use sports psychologists as well.

Which brings us nicely to the next chapter and what coaches and caddies can bring to the game…

Chapter 11: The Caddie/ Coach

All professional golfers invest in coaches and caddies. A caddie on the PGA Tour receives a basic salary – usually around $1,000 to $2,000 – to cover travel expenses. They will earn 5% of the winnings if their golfer finishes outside of the top 10, 7% for a top-10 finish, and 10% when their golfer wins a tournament.

If you have ever hired a caddie for a round, I expect that you will have benefited from the investment, especially on a new and tough course. It has been said that a good caddie is about more than just carrying a set of golf clubs around! A good caddie is a best friend, a guide, teammate, strategist, and a philosopher who helps a player to make excellent choices that can help in winning the game. The only thing that they don't do is hit the ball for the player and pick up the trophy at the end!

For many professional golfers, the relationship with their caddie is key to their success and becomes a long term relationship.

WILLIE PETERSON - was at Jack Nicklaus' side for five of his six Masters victories.

HERMAN MITCHELL - was with Lee Trevino for 19 years and all six of his majors.

JAMES ANDERSON - was Arnold Palmer's man at every Open Championship. When Arnold skipped the 1964 Open, he picked up Tony Lema's bag - and helped him to victory.

FANNY SUNESSON - was the first great female caddie, helping Nick Faldo to four major championship wins.

JIM MACKAY - spent 25 glorious year with Phil Mickelson.

TERRY MCNAMARA - helped Annika Sorenstam to win 48 tournaments.

Many of the great caddies have worked with a number of great players, and I am sure that there is some poaching going on, such is the importance of the relationship, and what a caddie brings to the game.

The golf coach has a completely different role to the caddie. They are not on the course during the game; they are not even allowed to shout instructions from the side lines. Their role is to help the player prepare for the match before they head to the first tee.

Professional sport is a high-pressure environment; one shot can be the difference between a pay out of millions and one of thousands.

We have already seen that the complexities of the game give the player high levels of mental and physical challenges.

One of the key roles of the coach is to give the player unbiased feedback on their performance. In today's world, this is helped by computer and video analysis, but sometimes too much data can cause more problems than they solve - my "Indian Restaurant" syndrome. The skill of the coach is to reduce the "noise", get to the heart of the issue and help the player to understand how to change.

Having been coached myself, I always find it odd that the feel of a golf swing and the reality can be so different, especially when you are trying something new. To see this for yourself, just look on the first tee at any golf club. Every person feels they have a reasonable golf swing and that they are doing the right things, but you can see for yourself how good the human body is at adapting and giving us false information.

Therefore, if you want to get better at anything, you must get correct feedback, and professional coaching is always going to be the best way. This is because coaches are trained to see the things that you cannot.

While a coach does not need to be as good a player as the player they are coaching, they must understand the game, and will have often spent as much time studying it as the player has playing it.

On the surface, the golf swing is a relatively easy action. The club swings back then forward and makes contact with the ball at the bottom of the swing. However, when you add in the human body, there are hundreds of bio-mechanical actions, from the hands, arms, back, hips, legs and feet. These are all working together in a specific order, in an attempt to make contact with a tiny ball, and at speeds in excess of 100 mph.

One small error can be the difference between a perfect shot and a lost ball. There is too much going on for the player to be aware of everything, so the coach is there to help the player understand what is happening and get them to adjust their game accordingly.

The coaching relationship changes as the player becomes more experienced. In the early days with a beginner and improver, the coach will be telling and showing the player how to do things. At this level, the player is unaware of certain areas, and this is the quickest way to get the player to adopt the right actions in the swing.

Once the player has grasped the basics, the relationship changes into a more collaborative one, in which the player asks questions, and the coach provides the feedback and helps the player to interpret what is going on, offers support and sometimes challenges them to be better.

As the money in sport has got higher and the rewards for success increase, the need for great sports coaches has also increased. Any top athlete without a coach would be looked on as a bit odd. Although they do exist, most of the time this is because their character just does not fit with having external feedback, rather than a decision that outside support is not useful.

If coaching in sport has only really developed over the last 50 years, business coaching is very much in its infancy. In the last 20 years more and more top level CEOs in major corporations are being coached, mainly because of the enormous amounts of money that is at stake in these organisations. If a business coach can help a £1bn company improve its turnover by as little as 1%, that would still be a £10m increase.

Unfortunately, smaller businesses have not been so quick to adopt coaching. The main reason, I believe, is they don't know it actually exists, or what benefit that they could get from working with a coach. I think that there is also an effect from the point I made in Chapter 3 - The Players, The majority of players in business are Life-stylers, happy playing at the level they are. Only those that want to improve, become masters and build "commercial profitable enterprises that will work without them" would ever really consider investing in a business coach to help them achieve their goals. Just as only golfers who want to play the game better would ever considering investing time and money in a coach

I also think that a business coach is actually more than just a coach and in fact takes on the duties of a caddie as well. This is because they are actually working with the player while they are playing the game, and are very much by the player's side and providing support. Just like the caddie, the only thing that they don't do is carry out the work or collect the prize at the end. As a bit of fun, I thought I would therefore look at the similarities of the role of a golf caddie and a business coach, and this is what I came up with:

To carry the bag - A caddie will assist you to carry your golf bag, so that you keep the stress off your body and therefore help you to have more energy and play better.

In business, the clubs are the strategies that you will use to play the 'Game of Business'. You cannot carry all the strategies in your head and run the business. Your business coach must have access to all the strategies you could need for you to call upon, leaving you free to focus on playing the game.

To identify the best club to use - A caddie will know your game inside out, and know how far you hit the ball with each club. They will therefore help you select the best club for the shot that is needed.

Your business coach will help you choose the right strategy for the right situation. If there is not one in the bag, they can help you find a new one.

To navigate the golf course - The course is large and can be confusing to a golfer who is not familiar with it. The caddie must keep you away from dangers and show you the safest route to the greens. Once there, they will read the green to give you the best chance to make putts.

If you think a golf course is challenging, then the playing field of your business is downright terrifying. You cannot see all the hazards, the economic weather can change by the minute, and you have no idea who you are playing against. A good business coach will have played the game for years, so there will be fewer surprises for you and they will help you see the pitfalls before you stumble into them.

For mental and moral support - In a major pro tour, tour players have high levels of stress for 4-5 hours a day, 4 days a week, so their caddie is there to support them and keep them focused and can help the player to make vital choices whenever they are indecisive or feeling stressed. The caddie can also assist a player to stay positive after suffering negative emotions from missed putts or bad shots and help them regain the confidence to carry on.

Most business owners have stress 12 hours a day 7 days a week and this is where a business coach can really help you. There are going to be mental lows that you need snapping out of, and decisions that you need to make quicker. Your coach is also somebody to "high five" and celebrate with you when you sink your putts.

To clean the golf clubs and balls – The golf clubs need to be clean so that they are in perfect condition while hitting the ball, and it is the caddie's role to ensure that the clubs and balls are always in perfect condition and ready for the next shot.

In business, if the clubs are equivalent to the business strategies, these too have to be kept in top condition, as there are always new ways of doing things and what worked yesterday may not work today. A business coach is always looking for new strategies and checking that the ones you are using are still effective. Just don't ask them to clean your balls!

To offer honest feedback – The last thing a good golfer wants is to be told that their shot was good when they know deep down that it was crap. The caddie is not there to make the golfer happy, but to be honest and give sound feedback so the player can adjust for next time.

This is the part that most business coaches love. They can see things that you as the business owner can't, or don't want to. Every action leads to a reaction, and if something goes wrong, there is a reason. The coach's job is to help you identify what caused it to go wrong and help you to change or adapt your approach in future.

To keep the score – A caddie is not responsible for keeping the player's score, but he is there to check that the player is doing so, and double check the numbers if needed. Get your score wrong in golf, and you are out of the game!

A business coach will keep you accountable to your numbers and make sure you review them on a regular basis. If you don't know how to score the game then they need to teach you very early on. Fail to do so and you are also out of the game!!

To win the prize - A caddie does not do their job for the accolades. Most people have no idea who a player's caddie is, but many caddies stay with a player for a long time. The trust they build is part of the reason why players achieve the success they do. The caddie's pleasure comes from seeing the player pick up the trophy and prize cheque, and receiving their 10% share!

Likewise, business coaches don't need to win trophies to get their kicks. They would rather see a client make £1m than do it themselves. It is like seeing your children achieve far more than you ever did.

What you can conclude from all this is that you don't need either a coach or a caddie to play the 'Game of Business' or golf. However, if you want to play the best game you can, then having one or both will help you no end. Both business and golf are complex games in themselves, but when you add the physical and mental game that goes on, I hope that you can appreciate that investment in your physical and mental development will pay you back immeasurably, both in improved results and in the enjoyment of playing the game itself. Which brings us nicely onto the last chapter…

Chapter 12: The 19th Hole

No matter what level of golfer you are, there is always a sense of relief when the game is finished. Now you can head to the bar for a drink and reminisce about the holes and great shots that you played, or nearly played! The social aspect of golf is one of its major attractions after all. Even if you have had the round from hell, the people you are playing with won't judge you. They may have a laugh at some of the bad shots, but they will all empathise with you, and encourage you to forget about it and try again next time.

And that is a major factor with golf, there is always a next time. While a round of golf is finite, the game of golf is infinite. You can play it forever, and people will be playing it long after you and I have gone.

What makes it enjoyable is that you always have the choice whether you come back and play. If you have had 10 bad rounds on the trot, lost a load of balls and generally hated every moment of it, you don't have to play again tomorrow. Your world will not stop, your friends will understand, you will still be able to feed your family and you will find something else to do with your time.

Unfortunately, this is the area in which business is most different from golf. If you don't have a business that works without you or you have not built up sufficient funds to be financially free, you have to go to work tomorrow, and the next day and the next day. Eventually, you will have been running your business so long that you are now unemployable, and therefore can't just go and get another job, so you just go through the motions until you are too old to play and retire on what little you have managed to put aside.

Imagine if that was golf for you. Your life did depend on turning up and playing. If you did not play well, your family would go without, but you can't quit, because what else do you do? I am sure that this is how many professional golfers on tour feel, once the realisation kicks in that they are unlikely to make it to the big league, but they do still have the choice to move into a different direction, once they decide that competitive golf is no longer an option.

Unfortunately, business owners can get themselves stuck with no apparent options available to them, but the reality is that they do, they just have to reset their view of the type of player they are. As we saw in Chapter 3 - The Players, if you are not yet a Master of your game, and your business does not allow you to truly enjoy being a Life-styler, then all you have to do is accept that you need to work on your game and embrace being an Improver. Once you do this, even if you decide that the current business you have is never going to get you to where you want to be, you don't have to stop playing the game, you just have to put your focus in a different area. In golf, it is like hating playing links golf, because of the wind and the unpredictable bounces. Rather than give up or just put up and be unhappy, move to a sheltered parkland course. While you may have to learn some new skills, many of the skills you already have will be transferable, and because you are now enjoying the game again you will more likely put more effort into Improving.

Just like golf, the 'Game of Business' is infinite. It was around before you started your own business and will be here once you give it up. But unlike golf, there are no set rounds that finish after 18 holes. As I showed you in Chapter 2, the ultimate goal has to be building a business that can work without you and can ultimately be sold. But that end goal can be 10+ years away, so you need to break your goals down into bite sized pieces.

I have always found that 90 day goals seem to work the best. This is long enough to give you time to do things, but not too long that other factors can get in the way.

Once you get to the end of the 90 days, treat it like the 19th hole. Review your performance with somebody, friends are good if you just want to laugh about it, but if you are serious, get your Coach to review your progress with you so that you get constructive feedback. Ensure you celebrate when you have done well, learn from the failures and always have something to improve for the next 90 days.

Also remember to take a break from the game. No golfer plays competitive golf 7 days a week, 13 weeks in a row. It is very easy in the early stages of your business to work 24/7 to get it off the ground, and frankly if you are not prepared to do this then I would question if running a business is for you. However, do not underestimate the impact that this will have on your physical and mental health, and your relationships with your family and friends. Athletes will always prepare hard before a major competition, but after it they will give their body and mind time to relax and unwind. You must build these breaks into your life, because they will not happen by themselves. I often correct my clients when they say, "I must find time to xxxxxx", with

"you will never find time, you must make time"

Time of course is your most precious asset, and one that you have equal amounts of compared with everybody. Some people have more talent, others good looks and intelligence, but we all have 24 hours in a day and 7 days in a week. The reality is, successful and happy people use their time more wisely than unsuccessful and unhappy people.

You should therefore organise your time and be clear on your priorities. This is why goals are so important, because, if you have no goals, you have no priorities. When everything is equally important, nothing is important and you will get easily distracted, procrastination sets in and time is wasted. I teach my clients the benefit of a "default diary". Think of this like a school timetable. All of the important things you have to work on are booked in at certain times of the day/week.

As a business owner, you wear many hats, Managing Director, Marketing Director, Sales Director, Operations Director, HR Director to name just the big ones. If you have grown to a certain size then you may well have delegated these roles to other people, but you still have to manage those people. This is one of the main reasons people find it hard to grow, because the key skill they must learn is how to manage people.

As an example, think of your school timetable, what was always on a Monday morning? Bet it was double Maths or English. i.e., the most important lessons were always done first thing, when you had the most energy. It was also a way for many (me definitely) of getting the hardest and least enjoyable lessons done and out of the way. Wednesday pm was always PE (sports) to break up the week and Friday pm was something easy and hands on, like pottery etc. The whole week was perfectly planned to get the most out of the time available and the student. This is exactly how top athletes train; they break the week down into activities which give them the best chance of success. And so should it be for you.

Write down all the roles you have inside your business and outside, put them in order of priority and then book them into your diary. You will have to accept that your diary will often get hijacked by other people, but by doing this you should be able to assess their level of urgency and importance in respect of your own list. Saying "NO" is the biggest time management tip I can give you. Also, remember, the reason it is called a default diary is that it should always be your default that you return to at the start of the next week. Just because it got hijacked one week does not mean that you don't try again the following week.

Now, let's go back to how we started the chapter and ensuring that you get to enjoy your 19th hole. In your default diary you must make time to do the things you want to do. Playing golf, obviously, time with family, fitness and holidays, need to be booked in as far in front as possible. Nobody lies on their death bed wishing that they had done an extra day's work!! You have to accept that you will never get a work-life balance - the best you can hope is that they work in harmony. This is another reason why golf is such a great sport for business people - you can do business on the golf course. Societies and groups such as Fore Business combine the two perfectly.

The one area that always gets forgotten in the process is booking in time to think and learn. Human beings are great Do'ers but we are not great Be'ers, and especially if you have been running your business for a long time, you will be far more used to running rather than stopping to think. But, put yourself into a seriously successful business mind, such as Richard Branson. How much time does he spend doing things versus thinking about things, and the beauty is that thinking can be done anywhere, even on a beach or golf course.

I believe the secret to enjoying golf, business and anything that you do in life is to be clear why you are doing it and be prepared to change something if you are not. If at any time you don't feel excited about it and you do not know what to do, reach out to somebody, but preferably a professional coach, as they will be able to help you. Just as the golfer who slices the ball must understand that they can hit the ball straight. They may not know how to do it yet, but working with a coach will help them understand and adjust their swing accordingly. The only thing they must have, is a desire to be better.

Golf, work and life are just games that we play. You get to choose how you play them, so play the best you can. If that means getting support from a professional Coach then do it, you might surprise yourself how good you actually can be!

Acknowledgements

Throughout the chapters of this book, I have referred to some of the books and writers who have influenced me over the years. I would like to acknowledge these authors for the help they have given me in my journey.

Having said that, I would like to dedicate this book to the hundreds and thousands of golf professionals out there, whose love of the game keeps them supporting and pushing their clients through this challenging game.

Just like business, golf is a tough game and the guys and gals we see on the TV really are the crème de la crème, the top 1%.

But this means that 99% of all professional players are not as visible, but they are equally as important to the game. Those that work tirelessly in the clubs and driving ranges, in all weather conditions, ensuring that ordinary people like you and I have the chance to be a little better.

My main aim in writing this book is to get golfing business owners to realise that there are professional business coaches out there to help them build businesses that work for them and give them more life. I also want to make those same people realise that regular golf lessons should be part of the fun and enjoyment of the game itself. No matter what type of player you are, put a bit of time, effort and money into your development and you cannot fail to get more out of both these great games.

About the Author

Kevin Stansfield has been coaching business owners since 2006. Prior to that he was a freelance Finance Director working with a number of fast growth businesses, helping them grow to multimillion pound turnovers and employing hundreds of people.

Joining ActionCOACH, the world's #1 business coaching organisation, has given Kevin access to some of the best business and sports coaching minds in the world. This, together with over 25 years of collective knowledge from a team of professional coaches that now covers 90 countries worldwide, give Kevin the tools to help any business to break out of the "work for money" trap and build profitable businesses that can work without them.

Kevin is still actively coaching and has coached businesses from start-ups to 4th generation ownership, in hundreds of business sectors. He uses a variety of group and one-to-one coaching, offers programmes to suit each individuals' time and money constraints.

Kevin believes no business is too small, large, new or old to benefit from having a Coach, and is always willing to meet for a coffee, virtually or face to face, to see how he can help.

Outside of work, Kevin – as you might guess – is a keen single figure handicap golfer. He also plays competitive club tennis, and is never more at home than at the wheel of a convertible sports car or on a powerful motorbike.

More can be found about Kevin at
www.abc-solent.com

or just drop him a line or a ring for a chat!

E: kevinstansfield@actioncoach.com
T: 07720292032

Made in the USA
Monee, IL
07 July 2026